FUEL FOR THE MIND, BODY, AND SOUL

"BE"

JOHN AND MICK TOSCANO

authorHOUSE®

AuthorHouse™
1663 Liberty Drive
Bloomington, IN 47403
www.authorhouse.com
Phone: 833-262-8899

Published by AuthorHouse   10/26/2022

ISBN: 978-1-6655-7460-0 (sc)
ISBN: 978-1-6655-7459-4 (e)

Library of Congress Control Number: 2022919899

Print information available on the last page.

Any people depicted in stock imagery provided by Getty Images are models, and such images are being used for illustrative purposes only. Certain stock imagery © Getty Images.

This book is printed on acid-free paper.

PREFACE

First and foremost, we would like to thank all of those who purchased our first book. If you enjoyed our first edition in our series of many yet to come, we know that you will love this book even more. Keeping with our theme to share our "thoughts for the day" in our unique way with the intent to move each reader to intellectual thought and self-reflection, "Be" is a book of everyday words that embody so much more than their simple, traditional definition. "Be" is not a dictionary in even the loosest sense of the word, as after reading each of our explanations and descriptions, you will find that these words will enlighten you and unveil much more meaning, substance, value, and most importantly, more "Fuel for the Mind, Body, and Soul." Each passage is yours to interpret and bring to life.

DEDICATION

For Dad on his 79th birthday,

What began two years ago, my brother and I made a decision and a commitment not only to this journey to become published authors, but to each other. Now, after these two remarkable years of sticking to our promise and sticking together, we have just completed our fourth book. John approached me and eventually convinced me of this incredible opportunity to partner up in an effort to motivate, inspire and entertain so many great people that may be in need of (or just missing) one or more of these desperately sought out emotions. Our genuine yet peculiar writings are designed around personal inspiration using our own "thoughts the day" in the most unique, yet fun approach with nothing more than the unavoidable impulse for each reader to think, reflect, and laugh together. Each thought is yours to interpret and bring to life.

So, Dad, we wish you a Happy Birthday. There are so many references made in this book with you in mind, that of which you will recognize and remember a time that your parenting and influence brought us to so many of our interpretations. Not only are you a great inspiration and role model to us, but you are also the best father that anyone can imagine having. It is an honor to be your sons.

Dad, this is for you. We hope you enjoy this book and the many more that we will publish.

.... John and Mick

GENEROUS...

Whether it be your money or your time, your selfless contribution or charitable donation should make a difference for someone; meaning, it should matter. If you struggle choosing between the two, then ask yourself this question: Which matters most? The answer is always: THE SOMEONE.

HUMOROUS...

The saying goes, "Live, Laugh and Love." Ultimately, your sense of humor plays such an essential part in your ability to fulfill your life with all three. If you truly wish to "live" with someone and truly wish to share "love" with someone, then be sure that your humor brings laughter to EVERYONE.

COMPETITIVE...

If there is anything worse than being a sore loser, it would be being an even worse winner. Maturity will bring more light to understanding that 1.) winning is always great, 2.) there is no talent in quitting, and 3.) pushing yourself to do your very best and inspiring others to do the same will keep you ranked as THE TOP CONTENDER.

PREPARED...

One certainty in life is that it is impossible to know everything. The genius in accepting this fact is knowing that you can set a path for success, for knowledge, for fulfillment, and more importantly, for happiness. Map out your plan, evaluate your environment, assess your ability to achieve it, and then put it all in motion.

ACCOMPLISHED...

We have all heard references to people who are "accomplished" pianists, artists, writers, athletes, etc., all of which are very specialized talents with whom those people are associated. Whether you fall into one of these specialized areas or not, strive to become renowned as an "accomplished human being."

TIMELY...

Take a minute to think about how each of the following can make you feel and effect your mood: Waiting on medical results, waiting to get your grades, waiting to see if you get the job, waiting to get off the plane, waiting in traffic, and so on. Did you think of the words; anxious, nervous, anger, stress, edgy, irritable, etc.? Now imagine that someone is waiting on you.

SOCIAL...

Not only are we social creatures by nature, but the benefits are boundless; both mentally and physically. With that being said, it is still a lifestyle choice. Find yourself in the middle between being an extrovert and a recluse as both tend to be awkward. Once you find your place, you will enhance your functionality, memory, cognition, and most importantly, your happiness.

WELL-DRESSED...

Going out to dinner, job interviews, special occasions, having company, etc. are obvious settings to look your best. The occasions that may be regularly missed are so much more frequent. Stay home spouses/parents, having dinner every night with your family, and working from home are just a few examples. The key is understanding how often others see this representation of yourself. Setting the example for your children, your invited company, and your coworkers will be memorable. So, how do you want to be remembered? More importantly, dress up for yourself.

SHOWERED...

Of course, the act of showering is recommended daily. However, when is the last time you showered your family and friends with peace, love, and joy? One may pride themselves on proper hygiene, yet you may find that cleansing your mind, body and soul comes from the act of giving.

FRUGAL...

Does anybody really love doing more with less? Think in terms of what you say to people on a daily basis such as, "Love You," "Thank You", "Good Morning", and "Good Night." We use these terms so often that they are taken for granted. If you aspire to be wise, truthful, trustworthy, and careful, consider being more selective as to whom and how often you deliver such common terms. The result may be that the recipient may not just hear you...they may listen to you, believe you, admire you, and most importantly, model themselves to be more like you.

PASSIONATE...

Great passion has been known to bring great pain. But why? Maybe for the fanatical, the overzealous, the obsessive, and the stubborn; yet for the focused, the inspired, and ambitious, it should bring purpose.

ACCESSIBLE...

One of the best management approaches in business is to promote your "open door policy." A true "leader", whether in business or life, is consistently and methodically seen inside that open door. If you are granted and privileged with holding such a position, be sure that people in your world can actually count on you, even when you are not needed at that moment.

KIND...

Being nice, well-tempered, gentle, and thoughtful may afford you the designation of being "kind." We all wish more people could be included in this list, yet you may consider taking this a step further. Your generosity, genuine care, empathy, and most importantly, your humanity may afford you the designation of being "one of a kind."

FRIENDLY...

This is a human characteristic that we all should possess, but it's really not that easy. Ask yourself, "Am I honest, do I have integrity, am I trustworthy, am I supportive, am I an expert listener, am I cheerful, am I admired, am I helpful, am I thankful, am I reliable, am I fair, am I available, am I thoughtful," and the list of questions go on. Now ask yourself, "Have I failed to be any one or more of these?" Knowing that we all fail from time to time should never outweigh the countless times you have succeeded. If this is true for you, then not only can you consider yourself to be friendly, but you can also consider yourself to be a great "friend."

READY...

While this fundamental state of being seems to be recognized and vocalized by so many so frequently, it involves countless interpretations of its definition, accuracy, and likelihood. There may be only two philosophies whereby all interpretations may fall: 1.) a completed checklist of agreements and conditions along with preparation can be used to confirm that you are good to begin, and 2.) you will never be fully prepared, so just start. Either way, your best bet is always to give it your best shot.

WILLING...

Once you have decided to attend a specific event or join the company of a particular group, you may already have, whether you realize it or not, enlisted as a willing participant. With any instance whereby you are happy to participate, there is much honor having the "will do it" attitude if asked or required to something. Stand proud, as these are some of the countless occasions where your integrity, fellowship and teamwork shines through despite standing in the face of controversy, the fear of failure, and standing to blame.

ABLE...

Take sports for example: a dichotomy arises at a time (most likely later in life) where you may become mentally able, but physically incapable of competing at a high level. Although this is inevitable, never count yourself out. You have the ability to share your knowledge, experience, wisdom, morals, ethics, and genuine care to motivate people to move mountains.

STELLAR...

Just like so many like-minded people do, you may also look at yourself in the mirror and see yourself to be humble, modest, shy, or even insecure. This is a direct reflection of how seldom we promote ourselves, give ourselves credit, recognize our value, acknowledge our strengths, and celebrate our achievements. Before you walk away from the mirror the next time, try splashing that cold water on your face and look again. Then recall all of those things we seldom do for ourselves...and smile. Now do you see a whole new person? Not just a superstar, but someone who is above and beyond the stars. It's you!

FAIR...

Reasonable, open-minded, objective, honest, impartial, and clear. These are the qualities that define this extraordinary, human characteristic. This is such a decent, distinguished, and admirable trait, that it has become more and more difficult over time to see this in everyone you meet. It may be due to the fact that a quality such as this falls in between stubborn and weak. Embrace your ability to be flexible, a free-thinker, and an expert listener; you just may be unique in that way.

LISTENING...

Everyone wants to be heard. Those who are successful in their workplace, love life, social life, family life, etc., most likely have the qualities of hearing, understanding, relating and/or resolving some of life's basic and most challenging matters. Taking interest in other's challenges can be most rewarding to both parties, especially to those who like talking about themselves. A feeling of satisfaction, fulfillment and recognition can result from giving someone your full, undivided attention while being emotionally available and impartial. Think of how you feel when someone actually listens to you. Now put your phone down, make eye contact, and feel privileged that they chose you.

POSITIVE...

Positively start your day positive. What you do the moment you wake up can impact and set the tone for the rest of your day. Making breakfast for you family can never be overrated, nor should it be undervalued. Starting your day finishing even the simplest task will give yourself a sense of accomplishment and pride, as well as a great mind frame to which you have until you end your day. Continue finishing your next tasks, one by one, all day, every day, and make this your routine as opposed to a special occasion.

RESPONSIBLE...

Whether they be minor, major, voluntary, involuntary, to something or to someone, we all possess obligations. As a parent, a teacher, a manager, or even a friend, there will be a time when you are called upon to find a solution to what had become a challenge. Keep in mind that you are more likely to be accountable for what you do as opposed to what you think. Use your heart, mind, and soul to be confident and valuable, and your support will not only be mutually beneficial, but rewarding beyond imagination.

RELIABLE...

This is an undisputable two-way street. If you want someone to rely on you, then you must be reliable. The fact of the matter is you need to be considered a trustworthy resource for those in need. Your commitment in embracing this characteristic comes with an enormous responsibility, as your words of wisdom will move people to their decision or action. Still have faith in yourself that you are up to the task.

HAPPY...

Most likely, this is the most sought-after emotion by all. Everybody has their own, personal list that will keep them satisfied; nothing more, nothing less. Why not break away from the norm, try something completely new such as laying in the sun in the winter, do the Jumble every day, and come up with your own "thought of the day." Make tomorrow better and different.

INTERESTING...

You may look for something that is interesting to you, but are YOU interesting? Test yourself by befriending someone you don't know. This will give you a fresh and honest perspective about yourself.

GOOD...

Touch, taste, smell, sight, sound. All things that can be "good" to your senses. The reality of it all, is when you can come to the realization the YOU are good. The rewards are unlimited, extraordinary, and mutually beneficial. Your influence, whether it be emotional, physical, or psychological, are permanent as opposed to a sense of pleasure that lasts for just one moment in time.

ELATED...

What an intense feeling for all. What can make
the world a better place is when you take the
opportunity to share this feeling with those who
brought you to that elation. Your appreciation
and acknowledgment will bring them to that
level right along with you. This is an opportunity
not to be missed.

SINCERE...

This has nothing to do with being nice, biased, and/or one-sided. This has everything to do with being honest, having integrity, and using your heart, mind, and soul to achieve and share ultimate, genuine authenticity to those who choose you as their source of reason.

AGGRESSIVE...

Once you are convinced through wisdom, experience, education and honesty, then you are ready to move forward and attack your life challenges head on. When you find success in taking this approach for yourself, only then can you recommend to others that they use the same approach using their own passion in tandem with your guidance.

ENTERTAINING...

Over time, you may find that others only listen to the wealthy and successful. Be assured that we all have a characteristic that others will enjoy just as much or even more without being either. What you say and how you say it, should move people to another emotion such as laughter, conviction, sharing, loving, and so many more. It takes two to confirm that one of you is.

THOUGHTFUL...

Although impossible to stop, your internal dialogue can improve and enhance your choices in life, business, love, etc. Take the time to think about someone else, someone in need, someone who is hurting, someone who is lonely. Your sympathy and empathy can change their lives, just as your internal dialogue has changed yours. Then you can enjoy the benefits of thought.

COURTEOUS...

Consider the opposite which is being rude; doesn't get you far. When is the last time you chose not to be polite, chivalrous, or well-mannered? When you find yourself extending this mannerism randomly to others who were unexpecting, complete your service by saying, "my pleasure" as opposed to, "no problem." The difference is that there was never a problem, it was always your pleasure.

GENUINE...

Being true, frank, and honest will take to you places beyond your wildest dreams. It's a quality everyone should have, yet not all do. You do. Sometimes practice makes perfect.

ORIGINAL...

Everybody makes mistakes. The simplest interpretation of this in terms of being human and making errors, is once you make them, learn from them. The object of the game is to not repeat them. Make yours unique, expect and accept criticism, but always stay true to you.

FORGIVING...

As the saying goes, "To err is human, to forgive is divine." When you find yourself presented with the opportunity to do so, don't make a decision that is the easiest such as to hold a grudge. Accept others mistakes when they ask you to forgive, as one day, you may find yourself asking others for theirs.

TRUE...

It is most important to be factual, honest, correct, exact, proper, etc. in the face of delivering information to those who consider you to be a viable resource. Take a minute to reflect on who you need to be true to initially, consistently, and faultlessly. The answer is found in your mirror.

GRATEFUL...

Welcome the gifts that you receive whether they be education, inspiration, charity, money, or even a toy. Let them see how thankful and gratified you are with obvious and deliberate gestures without feeling indebted by keeping score. Saying, "Thank you" and embracing them in a most comforting way for both, as in the end, they will be grateful for you.

THANKFUL...

For every day, make the most of it. Enjoy the gifts that you've earned, and appreciate your family, friends, and coworkers. These are the first of many that can be an endorsement to you.

APPRECIATIVE...

Life is short, so maximize your stay. Your value will rise among others based on your journey, your life story, your time spent with friends and family, and so many other favorable experiences throughout your life. However, if you choose to share your memories, it is important to be humble regardless of how much, how many and two what extent you value yourself.

GIVING...

It is much more gratifying to be generous with your sharing than to be gracious with receiving. Test the waters with spending time with those who may be running short, bring food to those who are hungry, bring light to those who are blinded, bring laughter to those in sadness, and bring peace to those who are struggling. These are the gifts that last a lifetime and need no special occasion to open.

TENDER-HEARTED...

Be gentle with your touch, be kind with your words, be selective with your actions. Each encounter matters just as much to the receiver as it does to you as the giver. Most importantly, be compassionate, as they will remember how you made them feel more than your touch felt, words spoken, and actions taken.

NON-JUDGMENTAL...

Open the book, don't decide its value from the cover. Open your eyes, don't engage based on one's clothing. Open your mind, don't close the door based on the first sign of opposition. Remember; there will come a time where you will also be judged.

ACCEPTING...

Sticking to your routine can be extremely important in finding success each day. If you find that this is becoming more and more mundane, you may want to seek or allow more opinions and critique. Although you will find that everyone has a strong and/or different opinion, keep your mind open while you attempt to understand. Whether you agree or disagree, find value in each; they were important enough for them to share with you.

BOLD...

This has nothing to do with being arrogant, loud, stubborn, or egotistical. It has everything to do with being confident, brave, valiant, and daring. This characteristic can be directly associated with being knowledgeable to help solve problems, being fearless to voice your opinion, being honorable by standing strongly behind your beliefs, and being adventurous to do things out of your comfort zone.

CONFIDENT...

Self-assurance is the result, but it is not innate. It is not even learned, it is simply acquired and built over time throughout your life. It is knowing that you are teaching a learnable lesson, nurturing a budding flower, sharing a contagious smile, and bringing comfort and love to a developing home. It's not just in your head, it's in your speech, demeanor, and actions making this a forever work in progress.

EGOTISTICAL...

This has nothing to do with being self-centered, selfish, arrogant, or even narcissistic. It has everything to do with being proud of your morals, ethics, and standards. One must keep these separate and distinguished, as this needs to be a positive connotation when used properly. Use it to your advantage along with humility, dignity, and respect.

MENTORING...

One must seek knowledge to find wisdom. Although you may teach yourself at times, there will be countless occasions where you will require someone to teach you. These may become the most important lessons in life. One cannot be satisfied with simply retaining this knowledge, as you are only halfway to the goal line. What you do with this wisdom can bring the ultimate feeling of self-fulfillment; and that is to share and teach others. Watch them absorb your knowledge, master their talents, and achieve their dreams and goals as a result of your gift of teaching.

CONSISTENT...

Your commitment to your work, your dedication to your friends and family, and your pursuit towards excellence should never waiver. It is the key ingredient to success in every aspect of our lives. Imagine your world without it; as you may end up right back where you started never once "passing go."

ENRICHED...

Enrichment comes from the desire to improve and develop yourself. In order to do this, you must first learn to listen and then act upon your newly acquired knowledge. A new life will begin surrounded by a wealth of knowledge, self-gratification, and peace in your mind, body, and soul. It is not a race; it is a journey whereby everyone can cross the finish line.

OPTIMISTIC...

Whether your glass be half full or half empty, you should have enjoyed the taste. There is nothing wrong with being the "devil's advocate" or having one in your conversation. However, even the mediocre people can bring out a problem. It's the brighter, more cheerful, and most intelligent among us that come up with the solution. The next opportunity that may present itself to you whereby you see the glass both half full and half empty, try submitting your solution first. It can start a trend of consulting you before anyone else. Believe the best is yet to come.

RESPECTFUL...

Knowing how to be should never be selective. Your character should include how you treat everyone even when they are not in your presence. Remember, if you are not part of the conversation, it just might be about you. Having class, etiquette, politeness, and consideration needs to be given in order for it to be received. Try to remember a time when you weren't, then ask yourself, "what could I have done differently?" Take advantage of this time of reflection, as it is never too late to make a change to that person you see in the mirror.

AWARE...

Although it is extremely important to use to avoid danger, it is just as important to be attentive to avoid missing something or someone. You may see someone in the act of excellence or maybe the last play that wins the game. Being mindful of your surroundings will always steer you safely in the right direction and lead you confidently to the correct decisions. Make sure you keep your eyes wide open.

CREATIVE...

Your originality, whether you know it or not, is in extremely high demand. Paint your own picture, write your own story, and sing your own song. Monet, Hemmingway, and McCartney never painted by number, quoted another storyteller, or remixed another's music. Once you learn to appreciate and utilize your own creativity, you can consider yourself to be in the greatest of company.

ENERGETIC...

When others describe you, do the words, "full of life" come to mind? More importantly, do those words come to your mind when describing yourself? Enthusiasm is not solely related to any amount of energy, nor should it approach being even slightly eccentric. It should simply keep your heart pumping and your mind sharp. A lively, animated, vigorous personality is not for everyone, yet it is powerfully magnetic. Maybe try using the stairs once in a while instead of the elevator.

TALENTED...

Everybody is in their own, individual way. If you struggle with discovering yours, find what you love to do, and master your craft. Aptitude and skill are not handed to you. Although some are gifted naturally, it comes with hard work, drive, and repetition. Without these, your ability to perform those things you love will rarely be realized. Never stop searching for your talent, as one day you will be surprised at how and where you find it.

INSPIRATIONAL...

Recognize how much you are and share it. More importantly, find it in others and capitalize on the benefits it brings. There comes an incredible amount of responsibility with how you deliver yours to others. Therefore, use your wisdom and experiences to tell your remarkable story while you choose your words wisely. You will be astonished to find how fulfilling this will be to all parties, including you.

INQUISITIVE...

Only those who are truly informed can consider themselves knowledgeable. Only those who ask questions, will be enriched with knowledge. Take a minute to reflect on how many questions you have asked the last time you needed information, and then ask yourself, "When was the last time you were interested in listening to someone else's story about themselves?" If you could spend equal amounts of time on seeking information about things that are interesting to you, find interest in those who have lived a lifetime more than you. You will be astonished to find that they may have answers to so many of your original questions, and you might just be thanked for caring.

COMPASSIONATE...

It's not just an activity, it is a heartfelt emotion. Make it a staple in your life, as this is so greatly appreciated by all. Of course, this is imperative during times of stress, sadness, and dismay, yet consider conveying this feeling during times of triumph, success, and achievement. Recognize their hard work, dedication to their art, and commitment to doing whatever it takes to achieve their goals. One day you may be part of that "Team" that shows it to each other yet have that unique part of life that only you and they can share. Go for the gold.

COURAGEOUS...

Nobody needs The Wizard to find the nerve. We found that the man behind the curtain did not just gift valor to the king of the jungle, he recalled each and every time through his journey in which he showed courage. Push yourself and find opportunities to showcase your bravery or stop and rewind your movie to see yourself as the king of your own jungle. What makes these times of reflection even more surprising yet amazing, as you will see others in each scene who you carried through those steps of danger during their time of vulnerability. It was you that was the Lion, so where your badge of courage proudly.

HUMBLE...

Nobody wants to hear how great you think you are. If you want to show off, do so with, self-reflection, modest affirmations, and thoughtful actions. Fewer words can be so much more impactful than many. Be calm, cool, and collected.

ROMANTIC...

Take the time and effort to study what your partner loves. It could be as simple as having "date night", quite dinners, and alone time together. Surprises have a proper place and time, so make them special. Be creative and make it memorable, as it should be exhilarating for both.

TOLERANT...

We are all subject to times, behavior, opinions, and conditions with which we simply just do not agree. Your ability to keep your cool, show restraint, and not allow yourself to take adverse reaction may take more than patience alone. Accepting differences in each of these in others is the first step in improving self-control along with enhancing your capacity to endure that of which may boil your blood. Your opinion should be kept as yours until you are called upon to opine. Just remember, your opposite behavior and opinions bring adverse reactions to some who are not able to keep their cool, show restraint, and keep their opinion to themselves.

COMICAL...

Laughter is the best medicine. Use your comedy responsibly. Jokes, funny faces, harmless pranks are just a few examples. Be sure to tailor these to your audience, as when you plan to be funny, everybody should be laughing. Never stop even when no one chuckles.

RESOLVING...

The first step in making mistakes, is admitting that you made one. This is neither the time nor place for egoism, stubbornness, arrogance, or selfishness in your course for correction. In reality, this is the time and place for the exact opposite behavior. Be determined and unwavering in your pursuit for an answer. Open-mindedness, teamwork, consideration, and compromise are all that is needed to succeed. Being considered a trustworthy, reliable resource for resolution is the goal. Be the exception, not a statistic.

HUMAN...

We all are, and to err is. To be one is a gift. Everyone is original, so make YOU count. Support everyone regardless of Sexual Orientation, Race, Color, Creed as these truly make up what we call humanity. So, appreciate humankind, as we all have this in common. Collectively do your part to make the world a better place; there is only one race...the human one.

SPONTANEOUS...

Just for one night, take a chance, change the date on your To Do List to tomorrow, cross out your plans, and get some sleep. When you wake up, decide to do something unusual, out of character, and unplanned. Right at the spur of that moment without hesitation, try doing something such as: make an impulse purchase, take an unplanned road trip, buy the first car you look at, play hooky, have a cocktail, or skinny dip. If you truly need a routine in your life, start by being spontaneous on Mondays. Either way, just go with it.

TENACIOUS...

Without the need for listing the right time and place for its role, your determination will lead to success in almost every aspect of life. Firmness, being driven, persistency, not giving up, never saying never, not settling for second best, and being goal minded affords you the highest probabilities for realizing your potential and reaching the stars. Stop and think about what you haven't done...yet. Do everything in your power to obtain tenacity and seize the day.

HONORING...

Our Country, Our Military, Our Parents, Our Partners, Our Ideas, Our USA Flag, Our Neighbors, Our Family and Friends, Our First Responders, Our Doctors and Nurses, Our Teachers, and Our Public Servants; Honor is by far, the most important word essential to understanding the most high-ranking emotion of respect, esteem, and admiration. It is one that should never be used loosely, as those people, places and things who are deserving of it have undisputedly and unarguably earned it.

HARMONIOUS...

It does not solely pertain to music; more importantly, it relates to a peaceful existence. Although Utopia may be imaginary, it should never be excluded from our mission and work towards living life in peace both internally and universally. One must find their inner peace before their ability share the wonder. Innately, we all begin life with harmony in our hearts, yet much diversity amongst our neighbors warrants a colossal, unified effort to convince the masses that a Utopian Society can actually exist. Attempt the impossible, change the world one person at a time.

AMBITIOUS...

Setting goals is not just for the business minded. Life is not easy, so it takes determination, motivation, and perspiration to make life fascinating. Whether you were gifted with the "go get 'em" attitude or you worked hard to get it, your goals need to be in the written form. Striving to achieve your wishes and dreams with ruthless determination starts with focusing on your target. Take darts for example, if you were blindfolded, do you think you can hit the bullseye? So how can you hit your goals if you cannot see them. Write them down, yearly, list those with whom you can work with to achieve them, pronounce the reward for hitting them, then drive hard, fast, and safe to accomplish your plan in mind.

TRUSTWORTHY...

It is imperative to have this characteristic in your portfolio of many. First, for yourself, yet more so for others. Do it consistently, and it will soon become natural. Whether it be family, friends, or coworkers, it is a moral that you can demonstrate and spread to others. It is not that difficult to do, so instill this in your daily repertoire. If you break it down, it is actually a two-part word: trust and worthy. The first part will inevitably lead to the latter.

ORGANIZED...

Plan your work carefully first, as this will set you up for success in working your plan. Not only is this important to do at work, but even more importantly to do this in life. Structure makes all things easier and will also save the most valuable commodity you possess, your time. Begin with this from the moment you wake up until the time you go to bed. It will surely reward you with a good night sleep.

ENDEARING...

How attractive you think you are, should be the least of your qualities. It's your charm and cheerful outlook that should be most appealing. Winning the hearts of others may not be regarded as the highest of priorities, yet you may hear yourself or others say, "I am not here to make friends." Understood, so ask yourself (and maybe those others), "Are you here to make enemies?" Having that winning attitude and magnetic personality can not only make you "likeable" as a person, but it can also make you "loveable" as a human being.

DREAMING...

It usually happens at night, so fulfill them each and every day. Enjoy your fulfillment and look forward to going to bed each and every night. Never stop, however if you don't dream one night, sleep well. Remember, you cannot control your dreams, but you can make them come to fruition.

BUSY...

As the saying goes, "If you want something done, give it to the busy person." Think about how many times your workload was heavier than your colleagues'. If countless, be honored, humbled, and flattered. Somehow your hard work is rewarded by more work, making you trustworthy, reliable, accurate, and in high demand. Although this should never go undervalued or unappreciated, take this part of your work home with you. Occupy your time so you never need to make up the seconds, minutes, and hours that may have been lost. So shut down the computer, go home, and get busy building your memories with your loved ones.

DEMANDING...

Start by being it with yourself, placing perfection as the ultimate goal. It will lead you to setting higher goals while ensuring that you hit them. Be tough but fair with others yet be prepared for any outcome. Teach them how you practice it before you expect their perfection. Always be understanding and patient with others and, most importantly, praise their accomplishments.

LOGICAL...

First and foremost, you must separate logic from emotion; meaning where sorrow and sadness starts, reason and rational ends. The challenge is to persuade and ultimately prove that these can be reversed. Emotions are extreme feelings of passion that move people to decisions less than what could be considered reasonable or sound. The proof is in the work and tangible facts that significantly outweigh feelings of attachment and loss, resulting in more sensible, analytical, and plausible decisions that may not be obvious to anyone but you. Tread lightly, as comfort and familiarity can prevail with lifechanging decisions.

THOROUGH...

Being complete means leaving no stone unturned. Do not miss anything, as you might just miss out on the best part. You don't read a book and stop reading before the last chapter; finish your book. Whether it is a task at work or living life at the fullest, leave nothing on the table. There is a great feeling of satisfaction hitting every item on your checklist; especially when you are done.

PRODUCTIVE...

With time being your most precious commodity, there is so little to be wasted. Before focusing on the task at hand, one should prioritize what is most important at that particular moment. Take your job out of this equation, since this is the most obvious, and consider what you do on your day off. Try knocking off your chores before anyone else gets up to start their day. If a choice of which of those needs to be made, "eat the ugly frog first"; meaning take on the most difficult or disliked chore first to get it off your list in an effort to ease the rest of your morning. Now you can create a list of items to accomplish that you, your family, and your friends will all enjoy. The reward comes when you check off every item on that particular list. Only then can you reflect upon your day and feel that you accomplished that of which you set out to do.

PRACTICAL...

This psychological characteristic falls right in the middle between being hardheaded and knuckleheaded. Unlike so many other measured comparisons of opposing traits, the distance from the center is colossal. There may come a time when you question if you are being realistic, logical, and sensible. Try asking yourself, "Are you focusing more on a theory or an idea that you stumbled upon in the past, or are you centering your attention on the actual sense of purpose and intended use?" With the answer, you can shorten your distance from the middle characteristic quickly and confidently.

OPEN-MINDED...

Opening is better than closing, specifically when it comes to your mind. Leaving room for opinions, comments, and criticism helps us become wiser. Utilize them all to grow. Have the patience to listen to everything good, bad, and ugly. Reflect on what you hear, yet do not let it discourage you. Turn it all into a positive using your reason, logic, and practical thinking.

SPECIAL...

Know you are and believe it. Find the specialty in others, as everyone possess their own. Make every day memorable as only you have that ability. Believe your friends and family are just as special and let them feel it. Your specialty can have an enormous impact on everyone you touch. items don't just come in stores, as the greatest one is life. Buy into it.

UNIQUE...

Have a quality that separates you from everyone else. This uniqueness makes you, YOU. Don't be afraid to don this hat. Never question being different as you should embrace it and endorse it. Originality is up to what you do. Take advantage of every opportunity and put on your own show. "Unusual" may sometime come with a negative connotation, except when it comes to you.

CRITICAL...

Although it may sound serious, dangerous, and desperate, convert this interpretation to be significant, essential, important and apply it to yourself. Your life journey has already presented you with moments in time whereby your choices had an enormous impact, influence, inspiration, and motivation on others in addition to yourself. These decisions and actions can set us forward or even back, yet you are forever improving your lifestyle and enhancing your wisdom. As you have already reached the light at the end of the tunnel through so many of these trials and tribulations, you are now in a position to offer guidance to those who are just beginning their journey unaware what their lifetime may bring.

LEARNING...

Everyone gets their education in different fashions. No matter what that fashion may be, it should never stop. Continue to gain wisdom in every way possible, as this thought-provoking process will help you mature both intellectually and psychologically. Knowledge is always available if you seek it whether it be found in a school, a library or through osmosis. Moreover, it is also learned from mistakes making it more probable that you will not make the same one twice. Teach yourself to keep your eyes and ears wide open. This is one of the secrets of success that is mutually and greatly enjoyed by the orator. Being taught is a privilege never to be taken for granted. Seize every opportunity that presents itself, as they most likely will be lifechanging.

HEALTHY...

Being truly "in shape" is two-fold; both mind and body as they complement each other equally. Rather than run through your day, take time to walk to see the beauty around you. Be vigorous with and stand by your beliefs, as you are the originator. Strength is not solely measured by how much weight you can lift. It also incorporates how you react to life's ebbs and flows, how you deal with your challenges, and how you react to adversity. Nourish yourself with knowledge, experiences, and time spent with family. Believe in your inner strength as others will see the muscle in your heart.

DEDICATED...

The price of admission for success and happiness is your willingness to take no shortcuts, hard work, and your discipline in supporting and endorsing your passions in life even in the face of failure. One must use everything they've got and leave nothing on the table. Our allegiance is not just to the American flag, it is to each and every person, place, and thing that our stars and stripes represent. Our loyalty is not just to a place of business from whom you are paid, it is to each and every colleague and client that supports your services. Our devotion is not just to those who we love, it is to each and every member of your family and friends that love you back. Be deliberate with your words and actions to show your pledge of allegiance to all who had influence in your life.

INDEPENDENT...

How many times can you remember saying to yourself (or others), "I was just about to say that exact same thing."? Don't to let that bother you, but rather know that you are in great company, with like-minded people, and you are among the wise. This is an indication that you are a freethinker with enough knowledge, common sense, and sound reason to be part of the solution. It is also an indication that it may be time to take the next step. That is to say that your autonomous path of thinking, although incredibly valuable, may be better served by linking with those like-minded people to contribute to the bigger cause together. The ultimate reward comes at a time when you alone, or you and your colleagues, share your wisdom with the students of life.

SAVING...

Take a minute to think about what is so important to you, that you would reserve it until the very end; or more easily said, "Save the best for last." The next time this opportunity presents itself to you, turn the tables. In the loosest interpretation, eat dessert first, pop the cork on that champagne tonight, or make the last dance your first. Just imagine if you saved the best for just one more minute, and you were a minute too late. Celebrate today, and savor tomorrow.

ECCENTRIC...

Maybe you already are, or maybe you have been told that you are. But aren't we all eccentric in our own way? Either way, look at the other members of this club to which you belong. Albert Einstein, David Bowie, Alice Cooper, Andy Warhol, just to name a few. It just might be possible that normal is boring, usual is monotonous, routine is mundane, yet our eccentricity may be criticized. Consider the source in the face of disapproval or denigration. Only those who cast stones are just part of a crowd. Your distinct, unique personality is one that stands out in that same crowd.

FAITHFUL...

Of course, a top priority for this should be your partner, however it goes way beyond that. Your loyalty needs to be consistent with those who play a positive role in your life. Being "true blue" should never come to an end, just as your personal encounters are never ending as well. Like the geyser, keep it flowing as faith should be a constant in your life, not a switch to turn on and off. It is personally rewarding in all aspects of life as it brings inner peace. It's such a wonderful feeling to hear someone say, "I have always trusted you", and equally as wonderful as returning the favor. Sharing the words of encouragement with others should not only be habitual, but it should also be imperative. Now add honoring yourself to your habits.

INFORMAL...

You don't always need a tuxedo and a podium to deliver your message. If your plan is well thought out, professional, and pertinent, you can do it in a t-shirt, shorts, and sandals. If you need to be formal, there is a time and place to dress to the nines and vice versa. Ensure that your suit and message are both tailored to the receivers keeping in mind that everyone understands laymen's terms. Fancy words are more suited for those working in the business as opposed to those of us that give them our business. Use common sense, intuition, and prior experience to decide what to wear, as it is YOU that will stand out, not your attire.

GRACIOUS...

Being courteous and kind may be a test on several occasions. Do everything in your power to be patient and pass the exam. Grace is beautiful to see in a ballet, but amazing when exemplified in everything you do off stage. There is never a special occasion to be cordial, it is always the time. To be congenial, it takes class, manners, and respect, especially when you host an event or invite company. Being well-mannered is your greatest support that is tied directly to your cordial behavior, just like tandem skydiving. Manners are a learned requirement. Take the time to heighten your ability to be gracious, and you will thank YOU.

COMMUNICATING...

This is a universal way of spreading your word, hearing others' thoughts, ideas, and concerns, better yet, sharing and spending time together. Every species does it in their own way, shape, or form. There is a reason for this; they would never have the ability to grow together, find commonalities, or say, "I love you." Words aren't always a requirement. Communication can be through expressions, actions, and body language. When you speak, you may say something you regret. The great thing about speaking, is that you always can say, "I'm sorry!" Choose your verbiage wisely, as people with whom you communicate are giving you the time to listen.

DELIVERING...

This does not strictly pertain to pizza, more importantly, your message. You have the drive to convey your point although not everyone will agree. However, they will better understand who you are. Knock on as many doors as possible, and deliver thanks, praise, and happiness. In the event whereby you are receiving a delivery, have your ears and mind wide open, and enjoy what you receive even if it is hot, cold, or late. Make sure you tip.

EMPLOYED...

It might be a tough choice if you had to choose between being paid for your professional services or being commissioned to a higher purpose in life. The fact that once you find yourself in high demand, this hypothetical question becomes irrelevant. Your service to society, family, and humanity may be considered labor to some, yet those who value their contributions perceive and embrace the feeling that this is a labor of love. Regardless of your professional path or philanthropy, change your train of thought from saying you are hired to "my services have been requested", you signed an employment contract to "my services have been retained", you have to go to work today to, "I get to serve a higher purpose today." Now it's our turn to add to this list. Employment is just your occupation, but being employed, or better yet commissioned, is a proud moment only to be retired by you.

SEARCHING...

Only you can answer for what it is that you might be searching. However, the unifying purpose of why people seek out their specific need or truth is simply find another a piece to their puzzle. The most common for which to search are professional or spiritual growth, support both in and out of the workplace, an emotion to move them towards peace, a sound decision, something or someone lost, and most significantly, the meaning of their existence. For most of these, a tangible answer that you can touch, taste, and feel satisfies and completes the journey. In regard to the meaning of life, there is one, universal answer for your consideration. That is to say that the meaning of your life is nothing more, nothing less, undeniably, and undisputedly, what you say it is for you. And other opinions do not matter.

STRIVING...

This is not craving, or any other adjective that describes a "feeling" for that matter. This is, plain and simple, an action. When one is determined and motivated towards achievement, it becomes acceptable to be ruthless, pushy, hard-nosed, and resilient in your pursuit. However, one must tread lightly and responsibly in the event that others become a roadblock of sorts, as the golden rule, "do unto others", should be followed. Never confuse "striving" with "starving", as the latter signifies a necessity that needs to be fulfilled in order to survive. Your strife should never be troubling, conflicting, or endangering, yet it can and most likely will require attempting, failing, retrying, and in the end, rewarding. Remember, there is no speed limit in your pursuit of success.

LIVING...

The question asked almost immediately by everyone at that exact moment they greet you is always, "How are you?" Imagine if the customary greeting was changed to the question, "How are you living?" The response would change so dramatically, as a one-word answer would not suffice. In addition, every answer would vary immensely based on their response reflecting on the present day, last month, last year, etc. I think we all can agree that this will never catch on. So, in the spirit of self-reflection, ask yourself how you would answer that question. Consider these prompts to get you started: Are you maximizing your stay here on earth, are you making life worth living (for you and for others), have you identified the meaning of your existence? Assuming that you may struggle with finding the truth within yourself to formulate your answers, it may be the perfect time to turn the page, reinvent yourself, create your "bucket list", and start doing that of which you haven't done...yet!

YOURSELF...

You are never alone as long as you carry your memories, passions, and dreams with you. Remember all the times where you touched someone's heart, or someone touched yours, you helped someone in need, or someone helped you, you shared your knowledge with someone unknowing, or someone shared their knowledge with you, you changed someone's mind, or someone changed yours, you made someone's day, or someone made yours. You are in complete control of you, and you are completely responsible for you. What you do with this is completely up to you but always remember: YOU MATTER!

Printed in the United States
by Baker & Taylor Publisher Services